A B HOUSE FOR KATIE

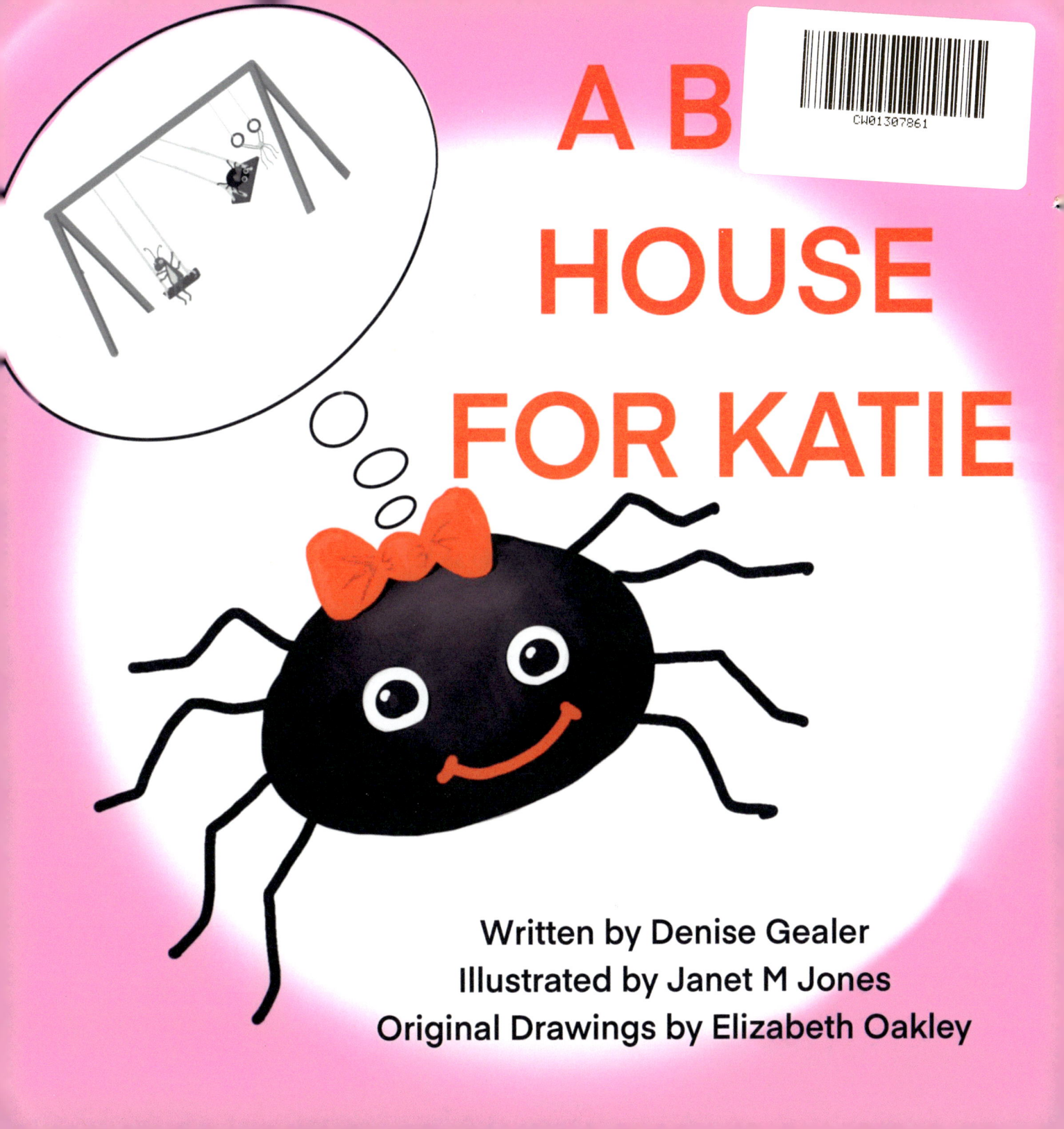

Written by Denise Gealer
Illustrated by Janet M Jones
Original Drawings by Elizabeth Oakley

A Bug House for Katie

Written by **Denise Gealer**
Illustration by **Janet M Jones**
Original Drawings by
Elizabeth Oakley
Copyright 2024 by
Denise Gealer
All rights reserved
including the right of reproduction
in any form
Manufactured in the USA
ISBN: 9798334569362

This is my book.
_____

Will you please read it to me?

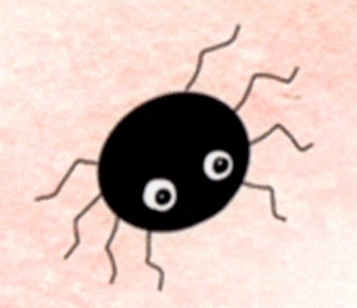

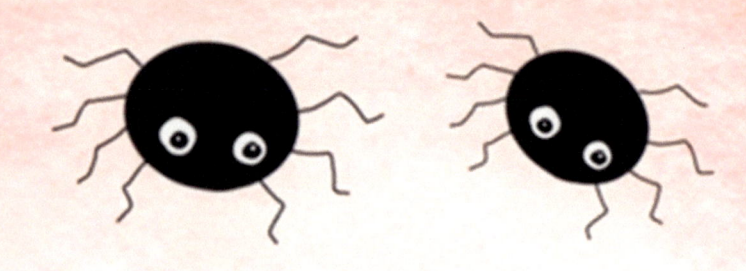

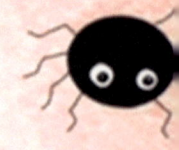

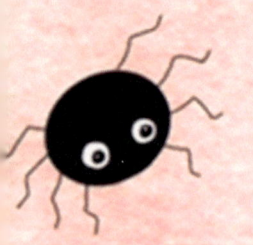

Dedicated to my children,
Elizabeth, Katie, and Michael,
and
to my grandchildren,
Emma, George, Ryan,
Teddy, Xander, and Allister.

"Mommy!" a voice shrieked from the next room.

"Not again," I thought. Mommy had just gotten my little brother Mikey to sleep in his room. My sister Katie was settled for the night, and I finally had Mommy all to myself.

Mommy and I rushed in to see what was wrong. "Mommy! There's a big, giant, spider in my room," cried Katie. "GET IT!"

"KWASH IT!" yelled Mikey, who had woken up and come in to see what was going on.
He's only three and heavily into destruction.

"It got away!" said Katie, looking very worried.
"Honestly," I said. "You two are so childish!"
But...I felt sorry for Katie. I hate bugs too.

Mikey lost interest since there was nothing to squash, and Mommy went to put him back in bed.

Katie's face looked like a storm cloud. "When I grow up," she said, "My house won't have ANY spiders!"

Well, that got me thinking.
"Gee, Katie," I said, "maybe there could be a special place under the house, just for bugs."
"You mean a bug house?" she said, her face brightening a bit. We took turns with our ideas.

"Yeah!" I said. "All the bugs would slide down a chute to a special place with wonderful things that bugs love!"

Wheeeee!

Ahhhhh!

Lots of CRUMBS!

Wow!!!!!

"And dark corners for hiding!"

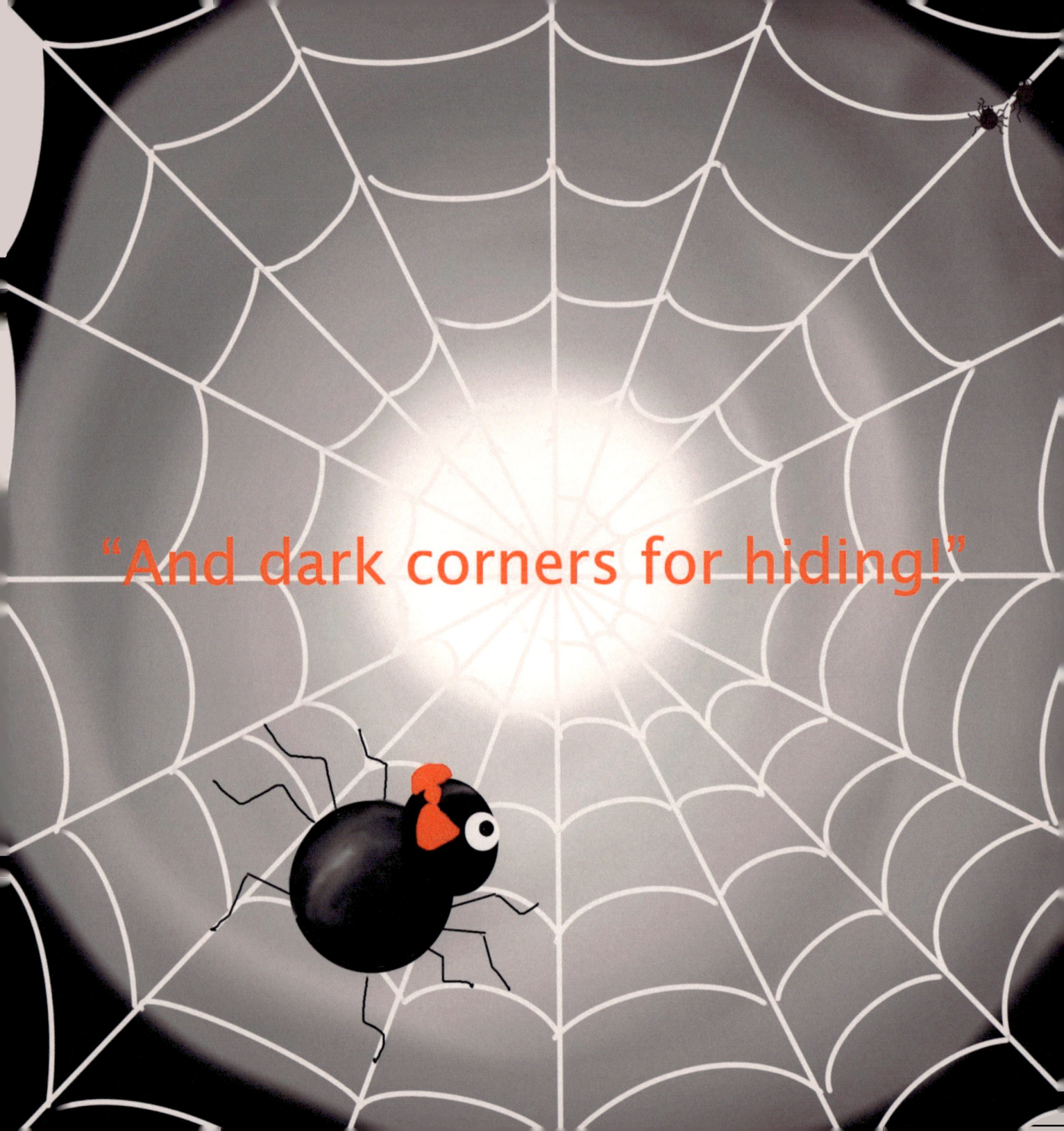

"RUGS!" Katie yelled.
"Rugs???" I asked.

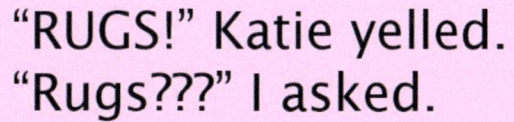

"Well," Katie answered, "didn't you ever hear the expression, 'Snug as a bug in a rug?'"
We both laughed.

"How about swings and slides?" Katie asked, as she snuggled back in bed smiling.

"And an indoor pool for water spiders!"

"Maybe they should have their own bathtub. They seem to like ours."

My turn!

"And a water spout to climb up!"

Katie and I started singing
"The Itsy Bitsy Spider."

"Hey, wait!" added Katie. "Don't forget a computer room!"

"They can have their own WEB site," I giggled.

Katie laughed, "That was a good one, Elizabeth. You're a nice big sister."

"Yes, and it would be sooo wonderful that they would never, ever, come up into our house! We can invent the Bug House and we'll be rich and famous!
Okay, Katie? ...Katie?..."
But when I looked at her, Katie was...

"It's bug happiness!"

...asleep.

So I went off to BUG Mommy.

THE END!

ABOUT THIS BOOK

I wrote this story in 1989 for a Children's Literature class I was taking at Bucks County Community College. Elizabeth was 10 years old and, with the help of her art teacher, Sharon Slack, she created wonderful illustrations using pastels. The pages were encased in plastic sleeves and bound as a "book" with long metallic shoelaces.

The title page, and the portraits in Katie's bedroom in the book you now hold in your hands, were lifted from the original version. Thank you, Janet Jones, for your amazing artwork, keeping true to the essence of Elizabeth's work.

<u>A Bug House for Katie</u> was shared with my kindergarten, 1st grade, and 2nd grade students for all 22 years of my teaching career. My students added some new elements like the computer room and the indoor pool and did their own illustrations for the whole story. Those pages were laminated, spiral bound, and added to the school library at Groveland Elementary in Doylestown, Pennsylvania.

Elizabeth, Katie (who still hates spiders), and Michael are now grown with beautiful, talented, creative children of their own. Now I have the honor and joy of sharing this book with my grandchildren, Emma, George, Ryan, Teddy, Xander, and Allister.

D.G.

Made in the USA
Columbia, SC
13 September 2024